UNCOVER HISTORY

ANCIENT GREECE

Rachel Minay

WAYLAND

First published in Great Britain in 2023 by Hodder & Stoughton

Copyright © Hodder & Stoughton Limited, 2023

All rights reserved.

Series Editor: Lisa Edwards
Series Design and Illustration: Collaborate
Consultant: Dr April Pudsey, Reader in Ancient History and Associate Director of Manchester Centre for Youth Studies

The text in this book first appeared in *History Detective Investigates: Ancient Greece b*y Rachel Minay (Wayland)

HB ISBN: 978 1 5263 2204 3
PB ISBN: 978 1 5263 2205 0

Printed in Dubai

Wayland
An imprint of
Hachette Children's Group
Part of Hodder & Stoughton
Carmelite House
50 Victoria Embankment
London EC4Y 0DZ

NOTTINGHAMSHIRE EDUCATION LIBRARY SERVICE	
E220237275	
Askews & Holts	14-Dec-2023
938	

Contents

Who were the ancient Greeks?	4
What was a city-state?	6
Why was Athens important?	8
What are the Greek myths?	10
What was daily life like?	12
What did the ancient Greeks eat and drink?	14
How did the ancient Greeks dress?	16
What happened at a Greek theatre?	18
When were the first Olympic Games?	20
Who were the Greek philosophers?	22
Why did the ancient Greeks fight wars?	24
What is the legacy of ancient Greece?	26
What to do next	28
Glossary	30
Find out more	31
Index	32

Who were the Ancient Greeks?

Greece is a mountainous country in southern Europe made up of mainland Greece and many islands. In ancient times it was known as Hellas and was home to one of the most well-known and wide-ranging civilisations in world history.

The ancient Greeks were people who lived in this area more than 2,000 years ago. Ancient Greece is often called the 'birthplace' of western civilisation because it was at the highpoint of western art, architecture, politics and science.

Arthur Evans

The Minoans were the first great civilization in Ancient Greece. Based on the island of Crete, their culture developed from about 3200 BCE. The Minoans became rich through trade and built elaborate palaces. An archaeologist called Arthur Evans excavated a palace at Knossos in 1900. He named the Minoans after the ruler of Crete, King Minos.

The Mycenaeans lived on mainland Greece around the city of Mycenae from about 1600 to 1100 BCE. Some historians consider them to be the first Greeks: they spoke a form of the Greek language and wrote using a system of symbols that we call Linear B.

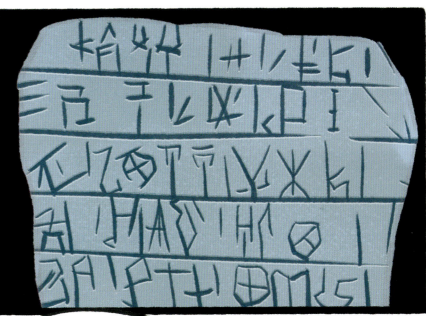

You're in trouble now, Troy!

According to the legend of the Trojan War (see page 24), Agamemnon, the king of Mycenae, led the Greeks to fight against the city of Troy, now in Turkey. The Mycenaean civilisation ended around 1100 BCE.

We know less about the period that followed, but there are more written sources from about 500 BCE Greece, a 'golden age'.

I've got a good feeling about this age!

This was a period of time when people made great cultural improvements. In ancient Greece, this is known as the Classical period, a time when art, architecture, literature, science and philosophy flourished.

What was a city-state?

Ancient Greece was not one single country but a collection of states that were based around a city or an island. Each polis, or city-state, shared the same beliefs and language.

The mountainous landscape made farming difficult, so most Greek city-states developed around the coast. The sea was very important – both as a source of food and as a means of transport for trading or war.

A city-state was made up of a city and the surrounding countryside. The major city-states were Athens, Sparta, Thebes, Corinth and Argos. All had their own systems of government.

City-states often went to war with one another but sometimes joined together to fight a common enemy. Athens (see pages 8–9) was the largest and most powerful city-state, but at times in its history, Sparta rivalled Athens.

Not many Spartans wrote texts that survive today, but according to the Athenians, Sparta was a city-state of brave warriors. Spartans considered strength and the ability to fight to be extremely important. Life in Sparta was very tough. Babies were examined by an official group of elders and those who were considered too weak were left to die.

We're told by Athenian sources that, at the age of seven, Spartan boys had to leave their families and live with soldiers to learn how to wrestle and fight. Girls and women were expected to be fit and strong because it was thought they would then give birth to healthy babies.

City-states usually followed the same design. The most important buildings formed part of the acropolis, which was always placed at the highest point of the city. There was also an agora, (marketplace and main meeting area) and a theatre (see pages 18–19).

City walls helped to protect the city from attack; the surrounding countryside was used for farming.

Why was Athens important?

By the middle of the fifth century BCE, Athens was the largest, richest and most powerful city-state in Greece. Hundreds of thousands of people lived in the city and its patron goddess was Athena, goddess of wisdom. Athens prided itself on being a great centre for learning and the arts.

Athens became wealthy because it was near the sea – which was essential for trade – and because silver and marble could be found in the local area. It used the marble to construct some of the most incredible buildings in ancient Greece, such as the Parthenon, a temple to Athena.

In Classical times, Athens would have been a bustling, lively city.

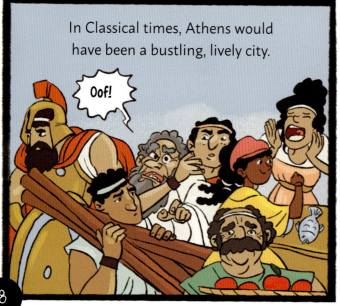

Many people lived and worked there while others came to study or to trade.

The agora would have been full of people buying and selling food, wine, enslaved people and horses. Men would also meet friends there to talk business or politics.

The various city-states had different forms of government. Some, like Corinth, were monarchies (ruled by kings). Others, like Sparta, were oligarchies (ruled by a small group of people). Athens invented a new form of government called democracy – or government by the people.

In Athenian democracy, the laws were made by the citizens, whether they were rich or poor. However, the citizens were men who had been born in the city and whose parents had been born there too – women, enslaved people and people from other cities were not allowed to be citizens.

A wealthy city near the sea had to protect itself from invasion, so Athens did this with a fearsome navy. Ruling the seas was necessary in order to survive.

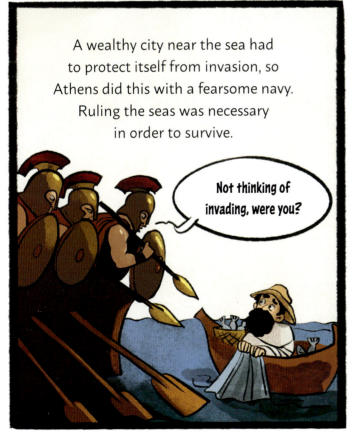

Not thinking of invading, were you?

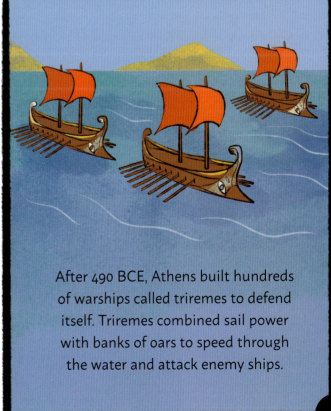

After 490 BCE, Athens built hundreds of warships called triremes to defend itself. Triremes combined sail power with banks of oars to speed through the water and attack enemy ships.

WHAT ARE THE GREEK MYTHS?

The ancient Greeks believed in many gods and goddesses rather than just one God. They used them to explain the world as they saw it. Their beliefs and stories about the gods are called the Greek myths.

Meet the main Greek gods and goddesses:

Myth was a big part of Greek religious life, and women in particular were very central to religious practices and customs. They could often be priestesses of major cults and shrines that people travelled far and wide to visit, like the Pythian Priestess of the Oracle of Apollo, at Delphi.

The ancient Greeks loved storytelling. They told many tales about the gods whom they believed could live forever. The Greeks thought they were quite like humans – for example, they spent a lot of time arguing! Some of the stories helped the Greeks to explain the mysteries of the natural world, such as thunderstoms and lightning.

RUMBLE!

Don't worry - It's just Zeus and Hera arguing again

The Greeks also loved tales about great heroes, including Odysseus, Heracles, Jason and Perseus. These heroes had to battle terrifying monsters, such as Medusa, who had snakes instead of hair and could turn people into stone, a one-eyed giant called the Cyclops, and Cerberus, a three-headed dog who guards the gates of the underworld.

Heracles was a legendary Greek hero. The son of the god Zeus and a human woman, he had superhuman powers and had to undertake twelve 'labours' or tasks – including killing the Hydra, a many-headed monster.

What was daily life like?

Daily life in ancient Greece depended on which city-state you were from, whether you were rich or poor and whether you were a man, a woman or a child.

Greek homes were built from mud bricks and had tiled roofs. Poor families had smaller homes with one main room for eating, shared bedrooms and simple furniture. . Richer families had bigger homes built around a central courtyard. There were separate rooms for different activities such as dining with guests.

Women and girls from families of high social status were expected to stay at home. Poorer women had more freedom as they could visit the agora to buy food or meet friends. Some Greek girls had a little education at home, but boys from rich families went to school at the age of seven to be taught reading, writing, arithmetic, music and sports. Many girls were married at about the age of 15.

Rich men worked in politics or as merchants, so rich people tended to live in towns where it was easy for men to go to work. Rich people also had enslaved people to do the hard work in their homes or on their farms. Some people were enslaved because of their skills and experience, such as doctors or scribes. However, most people in ancient Greece lived in villages and earned a basic living by farming enough food for their own family, possibly having enough to trade for other goods at the agora.

Rich people often rode horses, while the poor had to walk, but the mountains made travel difficult for everyone and going on a journey was risky. Travellers might face robbers or have to go a very long way round if city-states were at war. It was often quicker to travel by ship, but some sailors robbed their passengers and there was always a danger of pirates!

What did the Ancient Greeks eat and drink?

Ancient Greek breakfast was usually bread soaked in wine or olive oil. Lunch might have been bread with cheese, olives and figs. The evening meal was often porridge with vegetables, fish, cheese or eggs.

Most of the country was too mountainous for farming, but the hillsides were used to grow olives – to eat and to make into oil. In Athens, it was a crime to pull up an olive tree.

Farmers grew barley, which was made into bread and porridge, and sometimes grew wheat. Because there was so little rain during the summer, grain crops were sown in October to grow through the winter and spring. Farmers also grew fruit and vegetables, to sell in the agora.

Ancient Greek pottery was often decorated with pictures of everyday life. It was usually black or red. We know a lot about the ancient Greeks because a lot of the pottery has survived.

The rich in ancient Greece ate very well at times of feasting and celebration. A feast menu might have included roast pig stuffed with thrushes, a type of bird, oysters and cake.

Does that come with any vegetables?

A symposium was a party held by the man of the house for his male friends. On arrival, the guests had their hands and feet washed by enslaved people. Then they ate food, drank wine and discussed topics such as love or politics. Guests lay on couches and were often entertained by hired acrobats or musicians.

How did the ancient Greeks dress?

Surviving objects and paintings tell us a lot about ancient Greek clothes, hairstyles and jewellery. They also washed regularly, rubbed olive oil into their skin and wore perfume and make-up.

Ancient Greeks wore fabrics woven in the home from sheep's wool or a plant called flax, which is used to make linen. These fabrics were then made into simple tunics, which were belted and pinned in place. Clothes could be white or made brightly coloured with the use of plant and animal dyes.

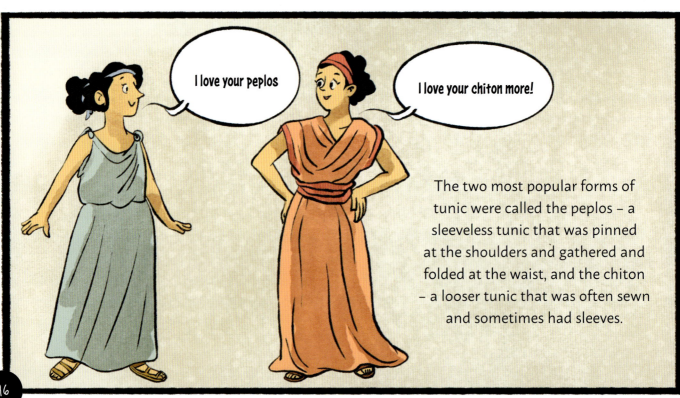

I love your peplos

I love your chiton more!

The two most popular forms of tunic were called the peplos – a sleeveless tunic that was pinned at the shoulders and gathered and folded at the waist, and the chiton – a looser tunic that was often sewn and sometimes had sleeves.

In early ancient Greece, the fashion was for highly patterned, bright tunics that were quite close-fitting. Later fashions were for plainer fabrics in looser designs. By the fourth century BCE, Greek style had changed back again!.

Both rich and poor liked to wear jewellery such as earrings, necklaces and rings. The poor might wear jewellery made from bronze or pottery; the rich could afford gold, silver, ivory and precious stones. People were often buried with their jewellery.

Footwear meant simple leather sandals or boots, although it was common for Greeks to go barefoot. It was usual to wear a hat with a brim to keep the hot sun off in summer. Both men and women might also wear a himation – a wrap or cloak that was thin and light for summer or thick and warm in winter.

As with fashion, Greek hairstyles changed over time. Women usually wore their hair long, but during some periods it was tied up with decorative pins, bands or ribbons.

What happened at a Greek theatre?

The ancient Greeks loved drama, music and poetry and a theatre was an important part of many Greek cities. Theatres were built in the open air and could hold thousands of people.

The idea of performing plays in a theatre began as a religious festival in honour of the god Dionysus. In Athens, this festival became an annual event that included processions, sacrifices and drama competitions. People started to build enormous theatres all over Greece.

A Greek theatre was built in a semicircular shape and the tiered stone seating meant that the audience could all see and hear the actors below. Actors were always men. A group of performers, called the chorus, commented on the action of the play by singing or dancing together in the semicircular area known as the orchestra.

Actors wore masks. The expression on the mask often told the audience something about the character they were playing. The mask's large features meant that its expression could be seen even at the back of the theatre.

Plays were either comedies or tragedies. Tragedies were often about gods and heroes and the main character usually came to a horrible end! Well-known Greek playwrights include Aeschylus, Sophocles, Euripides and Aristophanes.

As well as drama, the ancient Greeks enjoyed music, dancing, stories and poetry. The most famous Greek poet was Homer, who is thought to have written the epic poems *The Iliad* and *The Odyssey*. Lyric poetry was another kind of poetry, accompanied by a lyre.

When Were the First Olympic Games?

The modern Olympic Games are the world's biggest sporting event. The modern event first took place in 1896, but the origins of the Olympic Games lie much further back in history — in ancient Greece.

The first Olympics are believed to have taken place in 776 BCE and were held at Olympia in honour of Zeus, the king of the gods. Like the modern Olympics, they took place every four years. Sprinting was the only sport at the start, but others were added over time and the Games became a major five-day event. There were chariot races with as many as 40 chariots taking part at once; boxing matches, and violent wrestling events.

A modern city that hosts the Olympics has special buildings to house the different events and impress the visitors to the Games – and ancient Olympia did this, too. The Temple of Zeus contained an enormous statue of the god made from gold and ivory. The athletes had to take an oath and make sacrifices to Zeus before the Games began. The statue of Zeus at Olympia was so incredible that people considered it one of the seven wonders of the ancient world.

Only men could compete in the Games. Unmarried women were allowed to watch, but married women were not allowed to attend at all. This was because they were under the strict guardianship of their husband, father or brother, who rarely allowed them to meet or talk to other men.

The Olympic Games were so important that city-states were not allowed to go to war with each other while they took place. Men travelled from all over Greece to compete and winners were crowned with olive leaves and returned to their home cities in glory.

Who were the Greek philosophers?

Some ancient Greeks were great thinkers. They liked debating, or discussing, ideas about life, knowledge and their society. These ancient Greeks were known as philosophers, and their ideas continue to have meaning to this day.

Philosophy is the study of knowledge, truth and human existence. The three most famous ancient Greek philosophers were Socrates, Plato and Aristotle. Socrates was born in Athens and lived from about 469 to 399 BCE. He was known for using a series of questions to help someone examine their own knowledge and beliefs – this is now called the 'Socratic method'.

Slow down, Socrates! What was that last bit?

The reason we know so much about Socrates is because another philosopher, Plato, wrote down what Socrates said. But Socrates' new ideas were not popular with many people in Athens. Eventually he was taken to court for not respecting the gods and corrupting young people. He was sentenced to death by poison.

Plato lived from about 427 to 347 BCE. He was influenced by Socrates but also had his own philosophical ideas. It was Plato who wrote about the mythical island of Atlantis, which he said existed 9,000 years before and which in 'one grievous day and night… was swallowed up by the sea and vanished'. One of the things Plato was interested in was what made an ideal society and he may have used the story of Atlantis to explain his ideas. However, the mythical island of Atlantis – and whether it was fact or fiction – has fascinated and intrigued people for centuries.

Aristotle lived from 384 to 322 BCE. He was not just a philosopher but one of the first scientists. He studied many different subjects including poetry, zoology, politics and psychology.

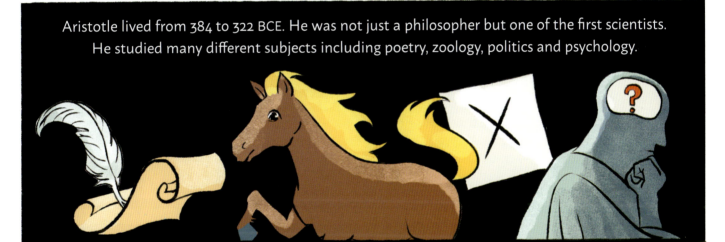

In about 387 BCE, Plato founded the Academy in Athens. This was like a very early university and Aristotle was a pupil and a teacher there. Aristotle also founded his own place of study, the Lyceum. Aristotle was one of the teachers of the powerful Macedonian king, Alexander the Great.

Pay attention, Alexander, or you won't amount to anything!

Why did the ancient Greeks fight wars?

The ancient Greeks fought many battles and wars. The rival city-states were often quarrelling and fighting with each other. However, they sometimes came together to fight against a common enemy.

The Trojan War is the story of Mycenaean warriors attacking the city of Troy in around 1200 BCE. The ancient Greeks told amazing stories about it, including the Trojan horse. Homer wrote about it in his epic poem, *The Iliad*. He describes how the Greeks secretly hid soldiers inside a wooden horse. At night, the soldiers crept out and opened the city gates to let the rest of the Greek army into Troy.

For many years, historians thought the Trojan War was just a legend, but archaeological remains near Hisarlik in Turkey are thought to be the city of Troy.

War was fought on land or at sea. On land, the most powerful units were foot soldiers known as hoplites who fought in a formation called a phalanx. Soldiers in a phalanx were well-protected by their wall of shields, but if a soldier at the front was killed, he was replaced by the man behind.

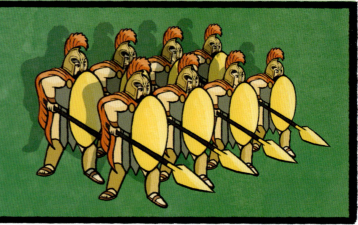

The best warship was the trireme. It was fast, with three rows of oars on each side. It attacked an enemy ship by ramming it, making big holes in its side and throwing its sailors into the water on impact.

During the fifth century BCE, Greek city-states came together to fight invasions from Persia, a vast empire that stretched from Egypt to India.

City-states were often at war with each other. Sparta faced Athens during the Peloponnesian War, which lasted for twenty-seven years (431–404 BCE). Sparta finally won, but within the next 50 years, most of Greece was swallowed up by the empire of Alexander the Great.

Alexander the Great was born in the ancient kingdom of Macedonia, in the northeast of Greece, in 356 BCE. He became king at the age of twenty. He conquered the mighty Persian empire and was undefeated in battle. Alexander's empire eventually stretched from Greece in the west to India in the east and south into Egypt.

Alexander was only 32 when he died. After his death, the colossal empire he had built up began to weaken and split. Greece would never be as powerful again.

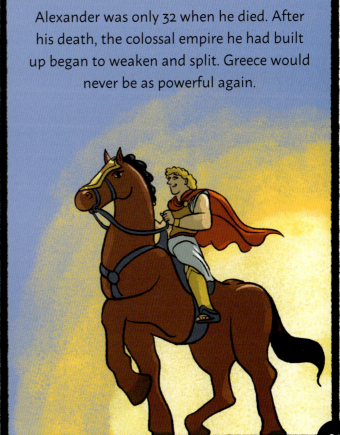

What is the Legacy of Ancient Greece?

Greece became part of the territories of an expanding Roman civilisation in 146 BCE, but the Romans adopted many aspects of it into their own civilisation. This influence has continued throughout European history.

Although the ancient Greek form of democracy was not entirely democratic – neither women nor enslaved people were allowed to vote as citizens – many modern governments are based on its principles. Giving the people a say in how their city was run was very different to one person (or a few people) making all the rules.

One day.

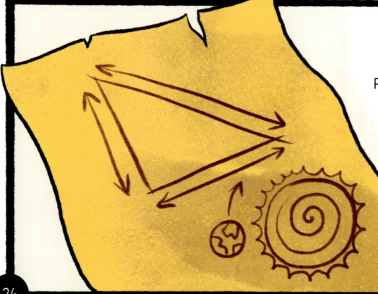

The work of Greek mathematicians such as Pythagoras and scientists such as Archimedes are still relevant today. Some ancient astronomers knew that the planets move around the Sun and how to measure the distance of the Sun from the Earth. They understood the importance of exercise, food and hygiene for good health.

Hippocrates is known as the 'father of modern medicine'. He believed in examining patients closely, observing their symptoms and treating the body as a whole. He and his fellow doctors wrote a guide for doctors called the 'Hippocratic Oath'. This still has meaning for doctors today.

The symbol of the hippocratic oath shows two snakes surrounding a staff.

The elegant buildings of ancient Greece were copied both by the Romans and by later architects. The Renaissance was a period in history from the fourteenth to the seventeenth centuries. During the Renaissance, people looked back at the Classical period to inspire architecture, art, science and philosophy.

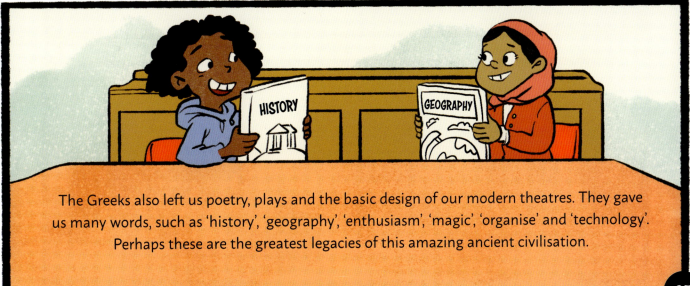

The Greeks also left us poetry, plays and the basic design of our modern theatres. They gave us many words, such as 'history', 'geography', 'enthusiasm', 'magic', 'organise' and 'technology'. Perhaps these are the greatest legacies of this amazing ancient civilisation.

What to Do Next

Now you've learnt all these facts about the the ancient Greeks, why not try and discover even more, using this book and other sources...

1. Choose one famous ancient Greek and find out all you can about them, such as Pericles, Alexander the Great, Hippocrates or even one of the gods and goddesses. Imagine what questions you would ask them. You could try making your own comic-strip story about them or even write out an interview.

Is it true you conquered the Persian Empire when you were only 21?

2. Write an imaginary day-in-the-life story of an ordinary person in ancient Greece – perhaps a girl growing up in Sparta, an enslaved person working in Athens or a young warrior fighting in one of the ancient Greek wars.

3. Draw up a timeline of the main events in ancient Greece, from the Minoans to the takeover by the Roman Empire in 146 BCE. Decorate it with Greek-style art. Collect as many pictures as you can to illustrate your timeline.

4

Choose one of the Greek myths. You could rewrite and illustrate the story or present it as a play. Perhaps you could even make Greek-style actors' masks or include a chorus to comment on the action!

5

Organise your own philosophical debate. You could choose a subject that might have interested Socrates, such as 'What is truth?' or 'What is beauty?' or you could choose a topic that relates the ancient Greek world to the modern one, such as 'What is the greatest legacy of ancient Greece?' Whichever side of the argument you choose to defend, make sure you do some research to make a good case.

6

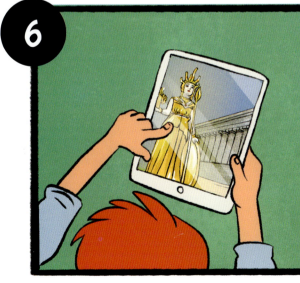

Remember to do plenty of research. Use your local or school library, and look on the internet. Also check out the local museums, to see what exhibitions they have.

GLOSSARY

Acropolis A fortified part of an ancient Greek city, often built on a hill.

agora An open space in an ancient Greek city, used as a market and a meeting place.

archaeologist Someone who studies the remains of past civilisations.

BCE 'Before the Common Era'. Used to signify years before the believed birth of Jesus Christ, around 2,000 years ago.

chorus A group of actors who speak together to comment on a play.

Classical The period of ancient Greek history from about 500 BCE to 336 BCE.

corrupt Influence in a bad way.

democracy A form of government in which the people have a say in how the state or country is ruled.

excavate Remove earth from the ground in order to find buried remains.

hoplite A well-armed ancient Greek foot soldier.

Linear B A way of writing Mycenaean Greek. Linear B was deciphered (decoded or understood) in the 1950s.

merchant Someone whose job is buying and selling things.

Minoan An ancient civilisation based on Crete, whose culture developed from about 3200 BCE.

monarchy A form of government in which the people are ruled by monarchs (kings or queens).

Mycenaean An ancient civilisation that lived on mainland Greece around the city of Mycenae from about 1600 BCE to 1100 BCE.

oligarchy A form of government in which a small group of people are in control.

orchestra The semicircular area in a theatre where the chorus performed.

patron goddess The guardian or protecting goddess of a certain place.

phalanx A block of soldiers standing or moving in formation.

philosophy The study of knowledge, truth and human existence.

symposium A party, often held after a banquet.

tiered With rows or levels placed one above the other.

trireme A fast warship with three rows of oars on each side.

Find out more:

Books to read

A Question of History: Why did the ancient Greeks ride elephants into battle? by Tim Cooke (Franklin Watts, 2021)

Discover and Do: Ancient Greeks by Jane Lacey (Franklin Watts, 2021)

The Genius of the Ancient Greeks by Izzi Howell (Franklin Watts, 2020)

Time Travel Guides: The Ancient Greeks and Athens by Sarah Ridley (Franklin Watts, 2023)

Websites

www.ancientgreece.co.uk/

www.bbc.co.uk/schools/primaryhistory/ancient_greeks/

http://greece.mrdonn.org/

Places to visit:

Ashmolean Museum, Oxford OX1 2PH

British Museum, London WC1B 3DG

Manchester Museum, Manchester, M13 9PL

World Museum, Liverpool L3 8EN

Note to parents and teachers:

Every effort has been made by the publishers to ensure that these websites are suitable for children. However, because of the nature of the Internet, it is impossible to guarantee that the contents of these sites will not be altered. We strongly advise that Internet access is supervised by a responsible adult.

Index

acropolises 7, 8
Agamemnon 5
agoras 7, 8, 9, 12, 13, 14
Alexander the Great 23, 25, 28
alphabets 12
archaeologists 4, 5, 17
architecture 4, 5, 8, 26, 27
Aristotle 22, 23
art 4, 5, 27, 31
Athena 8, 11
Athens 4, 6, 7, 8, 9, 11, 14, 18, 19, 22, 23, 25, 26, 27
Cerberus 11
city-states 6, 7, 8, 9, 12, 13, 21, 24, 25
Corinth 4, 6, 9
Crete 4
Cyclops 11
Delphi 11
democracies 9, 26
Dionysus 11, 13, 18, 19
Evans, Arthur 4
frescoes 4, 5, 14
goddesses 8, 10, 11, 24
gods 4, 10, 11, 13, 18, 19, 20, 21, 22, 24

Hades 11
Heracles 11
Hippocrates 26
Homer 4, 10, 19, 24
hoplites 25
jewellery 16, 17
Knossos 4, 14
Leonidas 28
Linear B 5
literature 5, 9
Medusa 11
Minoans 5, 17
monarchies 9
Mount Olympus 4, 10, 11
Mycenaeans 5, 24
Odysseus 4, 11
olives 14, 21, 21
Olympics 20, 21
Parthenon 8, 9
Pericles 9
phalanxes 25
philosophers 14, 22, 23
pirates 13
Plato 22, 23
pottery 6, 9, 15, 17

science 4, 5, 27
sculptures 8
Socrates 14, 22, 23
Sparta 4, 6, 7, 9, 25
symposiums 15
theatres 7, 8, 18, 19
triremes 9, 25
Troy 4, 5, 24
War, Peloponnesian 25
War, Trojan 5, 24
women 5, 7, 9, 12, 17
Zeus 11, 20, 21